GOD IN BETWEEN

Sandy Eisenberg Sasso

Illustrated by Sally Sweetland

Ryan,
Jesus says, "Where two or three
are gathered in my name, there
I am among them."
God is with you and we are for you,
Your friends at Willow Glen UMC

Library of Congress Cataloging-in-Publication Data

Sasso, Sandy Eisenberg.
God in between / by Sandy Eisenberg Sasso ;
illustrated by Sally Sweetland.
p. cm.
Summary: When two wise people leave their lonely,
confused town to find out if God really does exist, they make
an amazing discovery about where God can be found.
ISBN 1-879045-86-9
[1. God—Fiction. 2. Community—Fiction.]
I. Sweetland, Sally, 1956– ill. II. Title.
BL473.S264 1998
211—dc21 —dc21
[[E]] 97–38804
CIP
AC

10 9 8 7 6 5 4 3 2 1

ISBN 1-879045-86-9 (Hardcover)

Manufactured in the United States of America

For People of All Faiths, All Backgrounds
Jewish Lights Publishing
A Division of LongHill Partners, Inc.
Sunset Farm Offices, Route 4
P.O. Box 237
Woodstock, Vermont 05091
Tel: (802) 457-4000
Fax: (802) 457-4004

**To David and Debora
Rachel and Joshua
For windows yet to be opened
and roads yet to be traveled
—S.E.S.**

**For my whole amazing family,
especially Carson Dean
—S.S.**

There was a great and mighty wind, splitting mountains and shattering rocks by the power of God; but God was not in the wind. After the wind—an earthquake; but God was not in the earthquake. After the earthquake—fire; but God was not in the fire. And after the fire—a still small voice.

—I Kings 11–12

Once there was a town at the foot of a hill with no roads and almost no windows.

Without roads the people of the town had nowhere to go, and they wondered what was on the other side of the hill. Whenever they tried to leave their homes, they would sneeze through tall tangled weeds, tumble into deep holes and trip over rocks as large as watermelons.

Without windows they would sleep late into the day, and they often wondered when the sun turned night into morning. Their houses were closed up like boxes sealed with tape. They could never look out and their neighbors could never look in.

The people became tired of sneezing through tall weeds, tumbling into deep holes and tripping over rocks as large as watermelons, of seeing nothing and going nowhere, so they made their way to the center of the town to decide what to do.

One townsperson spoke up. "I have heard there is a God, and when people find God, God solves their problems."

"Let us find this God," someone shouted, "and God will build windows and roads for us."

Others thought it was a ridiculous notion. "People just pretend there is a God. If God were real, God would find us."

Yet the people could not see any other way to fix their town, so they decided to look for God.

But there was one problem. Without roads, the people could not go anywhere, least of all go searching for God.

They looked toward the edge of town where two old houses stood, each with a single window.

They called the man and woman who lived in those houses the Ones Who Could See Out Windows. "If they can see out windows," reasoned the people, "perhaps they can see a way to God."

So the people of the town sent the Ones Who Could See Out Windows to search for God.

The Ones Who Could See Out Windows thought that God must be on the other side of the hill, somewhere they had not yet been. They wove their way through the tangled weeds, around the deep holes and beyond the large rocks to find God. When they disappeared beyond the hill, some people thought they would never return.

The Woman Who Could See Out Windows went to a tall mountain. The climb was steep, and when she finally reached the mountain's peak, her body shivered from the cold, and she was breathless.

She gazed up at the sky and tried to tug on one of the clouds. She looked down to the ground and watched the earth spin in a dizzy dance, but she did not see God.

Then the Woman Who Could See Out Windows thought that God might be in the deep waters that covered so much of the earth. So she set sail on a ship that went far out into the ocean.

One day the sea waters turned from placid blue to an angry foam. A storm stirred up the depths and the ship tossed and turned on the waves. The woman imagined what it would be like to tumble around in the belly of a big fish. But as the ship swayed back and forth, she felt as if she had a whole school of fish in *her* belly.

The woman could no longer seek God in the ocean; she could only search on dry land.

Meanwhile, the Man Who Could See Out Windows traveled to the desert. He listened for God in the desert winds, and looked for God in the sands. The sun burned his skin and the hot ground made blisters on his feet, but he did not find God.

Then the man thought he might find God in the cool quiet of a cave. He searched in the dark for God, and he listened for God in the silence.

At first, the cave's wet walls soothed his sunburned skin. But then the black shade turned to thick ink, and he imagined scary sounds. The man became very lonely in the cave, and he did not see God.

The Ones Who Could See Out Windows were tired and decided to stop looking for God. Each hoped the other had been successful on the journey.

But when they met, the woman saw the man's drooping shoulders, and the man saw the woman's sad eyes. They knew that neither had found God.

The woman put her cool hand on the man's sunburned arm, and the man wrapped his blanket around the woman. It was a dark moonless night, and the Ones Who Could See Out Windows could see nothing but each other. In soft, small voices they talked long into the evening. They told each other their stories.

When dawn lightened the sky, the man said, "It's time to go home." And the woman agreed.

One of the townspeople was sneezing through the tangled weeds when he saw the Ones Who Could See Out Windows approaching the town. He called to the others, and they all came sneezing through the tall weeds, tumbling into deep holes and tripping over large rocks to greet the man and woman.

"Tell us," they shouted. "Where is God?"

The Woman Who Could See Out Windows told her story. "I climbed a tall mountain. I traveled on the waters that cover our earth, but I did not find God."

The Man Who Could See Out Windows told his story. "I walked across the desert sands that spread like a hot white fire over the land. I sat alone in a cave. Others have sought God in these places, but I did not find God there."

The people called out, "We were right all along. There is no God."

The townspeople's voices became louder and louder. They were so busy complaining about all the problems in their windowless, roadless town that they forgot about the Ones Who Could See Out Windows and about God.

Days passed and everything was the same in this windowless, roadless town except for one thing. The Ones Who Could See Out Windows helped each other put windows in every room of their homes.

Then the man and woman cut the weeds, filled the holes and cleared the rocks to build a road between their houses.

The townspeople were stunned. "We have never been able to have any roads in this town, and we have never seen so many windows. How did you do that?"

"With God's help," answered the Ones Who Could See Out Windows.

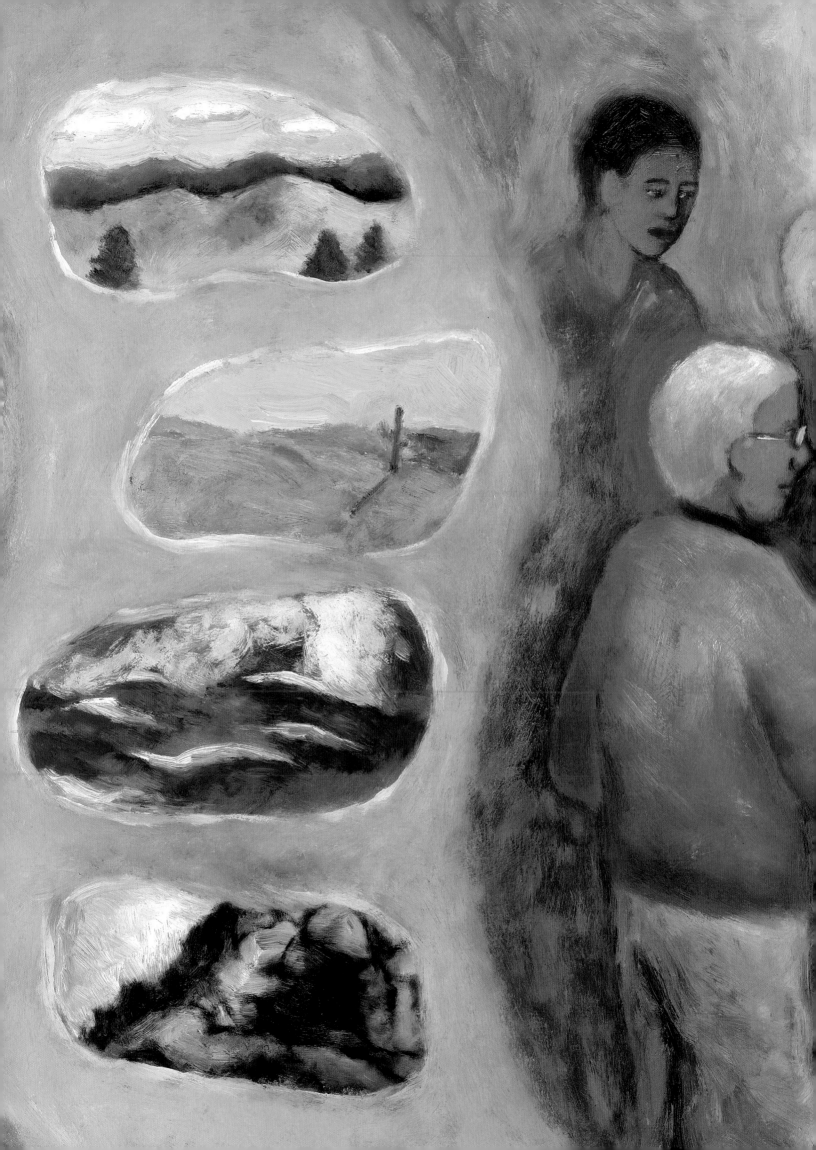

"But you told us you had gone to the mountains and the seas, to the desert and the cave, and there was no God."

"We journeyed hundreds of miles looking for God, and then, we found each other," said the woman.

"And we discovered God was with us," added the man.

"With you? Right here?" puzzled the townspeople. "At home?"

"Wherever we are," answered the Woman Who Could See Out Windows.

"What about what lies beyond the hill—the mountains, the sea, the desert and the cave?" asked a townswoman.

"Wherever we are," said the Man Who Could See Out Windows.

"But I can't see God anywhere," insisted one of the men of the town. "I just see you. If God is here, show us where."

The Ones Who Could See Out Windows spoke in a whisper. The towns-people gathered close to listen. The setting sun blushed the sky a deep red and a breathless silence embraced the town. "God is in the between," said the Ones Who Could See Out Windows.